Meggie Royer

"We're neither pure, nor wise, nor good; we do the best we know."

- *Voltaire*

always rub honey
into wounds
instead of salt.

i may have forgiven you,

but i haven't forgotten.

don't you dare think

that you can

make me unfeel.

no one ever told me
that sometimes
the best thing
two people who love
each other can do
is leave one another.

you may have
pulled out the knife
but you still left the blood.
it will be my war paint.

you wanted me
because i looked like her.
one day i will find someone
who wants me
because i look like me.

men live off our milk
yet they can't
stand the sight
of our blood.

i carry inside me
all the men
i've ever loved;
this is why it's so hard
to let you in.

it wasn't that we wouldn't
have been anything;
it was that you made me feel
like nothing
when all i needed
was to feel like something.

your hands are so soft
i almost forget
how easily
they could break me.

he looks at you like the moon.
if only i could be
even just one star
in his sky.

you weren't a bad habit.
you were just
the wrong kind
of morning after.

they all expect
to make me come.
i would prefer
that they go.

love used to look
so good on you.
but hate will
ensure your survival.

we didn't meet
at the wrong time,
just in the wrong life.

she awoke the ocean in you.
if you use it to drown her
I will make sure every last wound
you have in this lifetime
is filled with her salt.

i am not revolutionary
because i survived;
i am revolutionary
because i will ensure
that he doesn't.

how long

have you been waiting

for someone else?

return to yourself.

you have always been there.

there will always be another them,
but there can never be another you.
save yourself for the best.

every poem
is a paper trigger.
we shoot to kill.
forgive me
if our words are more blood
than ink.

my god, we could have made
our own universe.
but some orbits
are never meant
to stay in tune.

it's been so long
since i thought about sex
without a bitter taste
in the back of my throat.
you have to understand,
for some of us
there is so much distance
between coming
and letting go.

it isn’t your face
i’ll remember most,
but your silhouette.
it was more real to me
than you ever were.

if you leave me,
i will be the one
holding the door.

don’t flatter yourself.
i may have been
like butter in your hands,
but now he tastes like honey
beneath mine.

the next time
i open my legs
it won't be for you.
i have worlds inside me
and all you ever reached
was a single island.

any time you forget your worth
remember you were born
from blood and guts
because someone believed
you had the power
to be gold.

no.

i will not close my mouth

or my legs for you.

i have better things to do

than be soft

for someone

who only ever cared

about getting hard.

it's always dark
when you ask her to come over.
please stop trying to get her
to be your moon
when she can barely
even see her own hands.

we mixed gin with cherry syrup
and called it love.
years later
and your breath
still smells like loss.

you had so many snakes
in your basement
that the only way to kill them
was with broken glass.
now i know why
we broke up.
it was too much choke
and wound.

unlearning is so hard.
unloving is worse
but undying
is impossible.
stay.

no more poems
about how men
are like coffee.
i never needed either
to survive.

i knew we had ended
when i smelled her goodbyes
on your tongue.
so like brown sugar
that i almost wished
she would kiss me instead.

every mother in this neighborhood
warns her daughters
not to stay out past curfew.
pity that the men
don't have their own.

they will tell you to find someone
you cannot live without.
this is not sound advice.
the only person that should be
is you.

stage a funeral
for your sadness.
don't put roses on its grave.
sorrow is not like velvet.
it doesn't leave you soft.

vultures return to the dead
and not the living.
do not come back to him
when everything is already
lost & gone.

never run to someone
when you are lonely.
never make anyone
be your river
when all they really are
to you is a stone.

it doesn't matter
what star
you were born from;
it matters
how you survive
outer space.

listen.
there isn't an alternate universe
or another life after this
where you end up together.
but there are
other soulmates.
start looking for them.

he made me bleed
and then he made
me fall in love with him.
never trust a man
who can't
tell the difference between
a rose and its thorns.

sometimes love
comes in different colors.
but sometimes
people become colorblind
and that's
why we leave each other.

you give my heart
a hangover.
you give me
this honest urge
to get down
on my knees for you.

i gave so much
of myself away
that when the time came
to finally love myself
i had nothing
left to work with.

i think my body
is afraid
of being a body again.
it was nothing
for the longest time.

if you are oil
and he is vinegar
don't waste your time.
you can make rainbows
all by yourself.

revel in your ugly.
it will be ruthless.
it will make you afraid.
but it will save you.

CPSIA information can be obtained
at www.ICGtesting.com
Printed in the USA
BVOW08s0929220617
487581BV00001B/121/P

9 781329 794467